Help!

I Want to Start a Nonprofit

Small Business Guide

R.C. Marshall

DEDICATION

I dedicate this book to every entrepreneur that desires to pursue their destiny, be the change agent this world needs and give their life and **#unconditionalYES™**.

CONTENTS

ACKNOWLEDGMENTS

I acknowledge my husband Rick Marshall without you the pursuit of my dreams would have been impossible. Samara and Skylar, you are my motivation to go hard or go home. My brother Duane Ellis you have supported me in my dream and you are my number one cheerleader. Carol Burton, you are my unconditional love and support. My squad Monica Parrot, Tavis Taylor and Danielle Unique, you are my pusher. Shelly Lewis there are no words but, Thank You! Phillis Ellis (Mom) the reason I have gut and grit, you have shown my strength and gave me to the world.

To God without HIM I could do NOTHING.

Prepare * Plan * Pursue

This book is designed to provide information that will prepare you for the undertaking and avoid the pitfalls that can occur from a lack of knowledge pertaining to the nonprofit sector.

Prepare - You have already begun to prepare for the journey by becoming more educated on the task at hand.

Plan - Now is the time to create a plan with goals and objectives that will move you closer to the reality of running your own nonprofit. If you aren't financially prepared think about all the creative ways to produce the necessary revenue. I have known nonprofit owners that had a yard sell every week until she saved enough money for all her filing fees. Now her organization has an entire portfolio of real estate. Her mind was made up, no matter what hurdle presented itself she persevered. You must be willing to put in the work.

Pursue - There will be more road blocks than you will be able to imagine, however stay focused and remember your why. Surround yourself with other entrepreneurs that will continue to encourage you and provide great accountability. Never give up!!! You will feel like quitting but what sets winners apart from losers are those that have made up in their mind, success is not an option, it is a one way ticket. No turning back.

On my own personal journey there have been moments when I put my best foot forward, but only a handful of people would turn out. However, I knew I was born for this. My very first webinar was filled with people I gifted the class to. I didn't understand but I knew it was God. Well it was a test. The very next day I was called to teach my class on a platform with premiere speakers. What if I had given up and cancelled the class? I would have never been called up from the minor leagues to the major leagues.   Nothing that you do for God will be wasted. God is not wasteful. Trust his plan for your life and give HIM an #unconditionalYES™.

CHAPTER 1
NONPROFIT BUSINESS – IS THIS FOR ME?

Welcome to Help! I Want to Start a Nonprofit Small Business Guide

This book will provide essential knowledge to guiding a small business into the nonprofit sector. Before you take the leap into the business of caring for your portion of the world I want you to ask yourself a few self-reflecting questions. Make sure you think long, hard and reflect honestly. The nonprofit business takes a large amount of commitment and dedication. You must give this type of venture your **#unconditionalYES™**. You must have a made-up mind and understand with absolute conviction this is indeed directly connected to your divine purpose. It is at that point will you be able to have the self-drive and determination to go the distant to fulfill what God has ordained for you.

Ponder the questions below, search for honest answers.

1. Why do I want to start a nonprofit?

_____

_____

_____

_____

_____

_____

2. How does this align with my life's purpose?

_____

_____

_____

_____

_____

_____

3. What will be my nonprofit business focus?

_____

_____

_____

_____

_____

_____

4. How much time am I willing to dedicate?

_____

_____

_____

_____

_____

5. Will this be my only source of income?

_____

_____

_____

_____

_____

_____

6. How will I fund it?

_____

_____

_____

_____

_____

_____

7. How much money am I willing to invest to pursue my
   destiny?

_____

_____

_____

_____

_____

_____

Now that you have had ample time to reflect and have chosen to give
your **#unconditionalYES™** to your nonprofit business, it is time to get
down to business. I hope this question and answer process has given you
clarity regarding your thoughts as it pertains to questions that are crucial
to your success in the nonprofit sector. I will ask these questions again
after you have completed the guide to self-evaluate your perspective once
you have been provided additional knowledge and resources. Remember,
half the battle has been won when you decided to say yes. You are now
headed into a different leg of this race. Planning and to pursue your
purpose, by educating yourself and taking steps to establish your business
with a solid foundation.

This guide is designed to provide step by step easy instructions, from
choosing the most beneficial business structure, finding those all-
important funding dollars, to keeping you encouraged through the
journey. Now let's get started taking those steps to heal the world.

CHAPTER 2 BUSINESS STRUCTURE

What kind of business structure should I set up for my small business nonprofit?

There are several tasks involved with forming a nonprofit organization at varying governmental levels. One of the most important task is the business structure process. There are several types of business structures. Structures are standard across the board for, for-profit and nonprofit sectors. Below I have provided the general traits of each business structure; this will allow you to make an informed decision. Please remember ownership rules, liability, taxes and filing requirements can vary by state. For purposes of a small business nonprofit there is one business structure that yields the most benefit. That structure is Corporation – Nonprofit. Nonprofit corporations are organized to do charity, education, religious, literary, or scientific work. Because their work benefits the public, nonprofits can receive tax-exempt status, meaning they don't pay state or federal taxes, income taxes on any profits it makes.

Nonprofits must file with the IRS to get tax exemption, a different process from registering with their state. We will discuss the filings later in the book.

Nonprofit corporations need to follow organizational rules very similar to a regular C Corporation for profit business. They also need to follow special rules about what they do with any profits they earn. For example, they can't distribute profits to members or political campaigns.

Nonprofits are often called **501(c)(3)** corporations — a reference to the section of the Internal Revenue Code that is most commonly used to grant tax-exempt status. **This is the most beneficial reason you want to structure your nonprofit as a nonprofit corporation.**

While it is possible to form a non-corporate, nonprofit organization, and obtain a federal **501(c)(3)** tax exemption, the clear majority of organizations choose corporate status. Simply put, it is easiest!

Forming a corporation means that the founders, or incorporators, are creating a legal entity that exists wholly apart from the people involved with it. Most people prefer to form a nonprofit corporation, in part, because of the liability protection a corporation provides. For example, if a nonprofit corporation were to be sued, the assets of its directors and members are generally protected because corporate assets are distinct/separate from personal assets.

Business Structures

Sole Proprietorships
Partnerships
Corporations
S Corporations
Limited Liability Company (LLC)

Business Structure	Ownership	Liability	Taxes
Sole proprietorship	One person	Unlimited personal liability	Personal tax only
Partnerships	Two or more people	Unlimited personal liability unless structured as a limited partnership	Self-employment tax (except for limited partners) Personal tax
Limited liability company (LLC)	One or more people	Owners are not personally liable	Self-employment tax Personal tax or corporate tax
Corporation - C corp	One or more people	Owners are not personally liable	Corporate tax

Corporation - S corp	One or more people, but no more than 100, and all must be U.S. citizens	Owners are not personally liable	Personal tax
Corporation - B corp	One or more people	Owners are not personally liable	Corporate tax
Corporation - Nonprofit	One or more people	Owners are not personally liable	Tax-exempt, but corporate profits can't be distributed

Source (SBA, 2018) Figure 1

First Things First

What have you decided to name your business? Put some thought into it. How does the name represent the brand I intend to display? Have I prayed and sought clear direction? How does the name play into my plan for my website address? Have I researched the name to verify its availability with the state?

A nonprofit is a legal business that requires you to register your business with the Secretary of State. The Secretary of State web address varies by state. For the illustrations in the book I will be using the state of Georgia (check your local listing for your Secretary of State). For your state fee and document requirements you can check the link below.

https://www.harborcompliance.com/information/how-to-start-a-non-profit-organization

1. Go to the state Secretary of State website https://ecorp.sos.ga.gov/

2. Go to the Business Search icon and enter your proposed name. Review the results and this will give you an idea if there is a state business with your proposed name. This minimizes losing the name registration fee.   The fee is nonrefundable if you choose a name that is already in use.

3. Go to register a name reservation with the state to ensure your business name is unique. Cost $25* (price varies by state). Once you apply for your name reservation you will receive a reservation number valid for 30 days. This will allow you to register your corporation with the state for up to thirty days without fear that someone else will take your name. We are in business we have a name! Give yourself a loud shout out. You did it!

4. Now, onto the next step, it is time to prepare to register your business. I have included a sample incorporation worksheet. Don't let the worksheet overwhelm you! This worksheet will aid in preparation to answer the questions online. When you register online it will be a simple guided questionnaire (review your states filing option).   Please verify your articles of incorporation and bylaws with a professional, i.e. attorney to ensure you have filled

the necessary requirements on the state and federal level. It is less costly if you have all this information prepared in a worksheet if you are planning to allow a professional to handle your paperwork.

This process will also educate you on YOUR business. I hear horror stories of how people have paid thousands of dollars to have their nonprofit paperwork completed, only to receive an incomplete business filing status. Remember knowledge is power. You may not be able to do it all, but you will know what to expect if you seek outside counsel or assistance. Running a business often means you hold many positions due to financial constraints. However, invest wisely to ensure the legal component of your business is setup properly. A wise investment does not equate to overly priced. Seek out recommendations and verify references to minimize the probability of being overpriced and underserved. In the back of the book there are several references that will provide excellent services at a discount for purchasing my products.

5. Now that we have completed those articles of incorporation head back to the Secretary of State website to complete your registration. Make sure you have your documents, you will need them to assist with your registration. You will receive official articles of incorporation 1-page document from the state once your filing has been approved for your records (procedure may vary from state to state). Phase one completed! Let's celebrate. You are officially the owner of a nonprofit business. You are well on your way. You did it!

Do you need your board of directors in place before your paperwork is filed?
Yes and No. As it stands it not necessary to have each board position filled before your paperwork is filed, it is important that you have the board positions filled that will be legally accountable for the activities in your nonprofit organization. As a small business often your initial board is often the same as your officers.

Though officers are typically board members, there are no guidelines or requirements that suggest an organization cannot elect an individual outside the board to be an officer for the organization (unless the officer roles described in the organization's bylaws state otherwise). It is possible for an individual to hold two separate offices, with the exception that the President cannot also serve as the Secretary. This also means you can hold two of those positions apart from Secretary. At a later time, you can begin to add and reorganize your board of directors as you see beneficial for the longevity of your organization.

Do not let this item be a reason to delay your business filing.

The articles of incorporation — or a certificate of incorporation — is a comprehensive legal document that lays out the basic outline of your business. It's required by every state when you incorporate. The most common information included is the company name, business purpose, number of shares offered, value of shares, directors, and officers. This is relevant to a Corporation (any kind)

Bylaws (called resolutions for nonprofits) are the internal governance documents of a corporation. They define how key business decisions are made, as well as officer and shareholders' duties, powers, and responsibilities. It's widely recommended to create one to protect yourself and your business, even if your state doesn't mandate it.

INCORPORATION WORKSHEET
Sample worksheet

INCORPORATOR:

Name: Sample Business Name
Street Address: _____
City, State, Zip: _____, N/A 30316
Telephone: _____ Ext. _____

CORPORATION NAME:

Legal Name: _____
Trade Name: _____

PRINCIPAL PLACE OF BUSINESS:

The address where the corporation's principal place of business will be located is:
Street Address: _____
City, State, Zip: _____, _____
_____
County: _____
Telephone: _____

Mailing Address: _____
City, State, Zip: _____, _____
_____

BUSINESS ACTIVITIES: This corporation will begin on _____, with an initial number of employees of approximately 0, and anticipated first year gross revenues of approximately $0.00.

The primary activities of the corporation can be described as follows: _____.

GEOGRAPHICAL AREA OF BUSINESS OPERATIONS:

The business will conduct its operations in the following geographical area: _____.

STOCK:

The corporation will authorize the following number of shares: 0

The shares will be: no par value

The shareholders will be required to first offer their shares to the corporation before selling to other parties.

FISCAL YEAR:

The fiscal year of the corporation will end each year on December 31.

DIRECTORS:

The following persons will be the initial directors of the corporation:

The terms of the regular directors will be staggered and the directors will be divided into _____ groups. Each director will serve for a term of _____ year(s).

The directors will not be personally liable to the corporation or its shareholders for obligations arising out of the performance of the directors' duties.

OFFICERS:

The following persons will be elected to fill the respective offices:

President: _____
Address: _____
City, State, Zip: _____, _____
_____
Telephone: _____ Ext._____

Vice President: _____
Address: _____
City, State, Zip: _____, _____
_____
Telephone: _____ Ext._____

Secretary: _____
Address: _____
City, State, Zip: _____, _____
_____
Telephone: _____ Ext._____

Instruments which relate to an interest in real estate must be signed by the following:

President or Vice-President and Secretary

The officers are authorized to do the following:

Open a corporate bank account
Obtain a bank loan
Elect Subchapter "S" tax status
Lease office space at _____, _____,
_____ from _____ upon such terms as
the officers deem appropriate.

Employment agreements will be authorized with the following officers:

_____

SEAL:

The corporation will not have a corporate seal.

STOCK CERTIFICATES:

The corporation will not, unless requested, issue stock certificates.

REGISTERED AGENT: definition A registered agent receives official papers and legal documents on behalf of your company. The registered agent must be in the state where you register. You can be your own registered agent especially since you are a small business. Any legal papers you have issues understanding you can always call the governmental agency and they will explain your options or you can contact a lawyer. I would always call the agency first.

The name and address of the registered agent of the corporation is:

Name: _____
Company Name: _____
Address: _____
City, State, Zip: _____, _____
_____
Telephone: _____ Ext._____

ADVISORS:

The following financial and professional advisors will be providing services to the business:

Accountant: _____
Firm Name: _____
Address: _____
City, State, Zip: _____, _____
_____
Telephone: _____ Ext._____

Lawyer: _____
Firm Name: _____
Address: _____
City, State, Zip: _____, _____
_____
Telephone: _____ Ext._____

Figure 2

ARTICLES OF INCORPORATION
OF
Sample ABC Nonprofit

ARTICLE I
NAME

The name of the corporation is ABC Nonprofit, INC.

ARTICLE II
NONPROFIT CORPORATION AND CHARITABLE PURPOSES

The Corporation is a nonprofit corporation under the provisions of the Georgia Nonprofit Corporation Code. It is organized, and shall always operate, exclusively for public "charitable uses and purposes" (as defined in Article XI herein below). In furtherance of such purposes, the Corporation shall have full power and authority:

(a) To acquire and administer funds and property which, after the payment of necessary expenses, shall be devoted to charitable, scientific, literary and educational purposes within the meaning of Section 501(c)(3) of the Internal Revenue Code of 1986, as amended (the "Code"), as may be determined from time to time by the Board of Directors. The preceding sentence shall not be construed to require the Board of Directors to distribute the principal or corpus held by the corporation;

(b) To make distributions to organizations that qualify as tax exempt organizations under Sections 501(a) and 501(c)(3) of the Code;

(c) To make distributions to individuals for charitable purposes within the definition of Section 501(c)(3) of the Code;

(d) To receive and accept property, whether real, personal, or mixed, by way of gift, bequest or devise, from any person, firm, trust or corporation, to be held, administered and disposed of in accordance with and pursuant to the governing instruments of the Corporation, as the same shall be amended from time to time; and

(e) To perform all other acts necessary or incidental to the above and to do whatever is deemed necessary, useful, advisable or conducive, directly or indirectly, as determined by the Board of Directors to carry out any of the purposes of the Corporation, as set forth in these Articles of Incorporation, including the exercise of all other power and authority enjoyed by corporations generally by virtue of the provisions of the Georgia Nonprofit Corporation Code (within and subject to the limitations of Section 501(c)(3) of the Code).

The Corporation shall serve only such purposes and functions and shall engage only in such activities as are consonant with the purposes set forth in this Article II and as are exclusively charitable and are entitled to charitable status under Section 501(c)(3) of the Code.

ARTICLE III
DURATION

The Corporation shall have perpetual duration.

ARTICLE IV
TAX-EXEMPT NONPROFIT CORPORATION

(a) The Corporation shall be neither organized nor operated for pecuniary gain or profit.

(b) No part of the net earnings of the Corporation shall inure to the benefit of, or be distributable to, any director, officer or employee of the Corporation, or any other private person; but the Corporation shall be authorized and empowered to pay reasonable compensation for services rendered and to make payments and distributions in furtherance of the purposes as set forth in Article II hereof.

(c) No substantial part of the activities of the Corporation shall be the carrying on of propaganda, or otherwise attempting to influence legislation; and the Corporation shall not participate in, or intervene in (including the publication or distribution of statements) any political campaign on behalf of any candidate for public office.

(d) Notwithstanding any other provisions of these Articles of Incorporation, the Corporation shall not carry on any other activities not permitted to be carried on:

(i) By a corporation exempt from federal income taxation under Section 501(c)(3) of the Code; or

(ii) By a corporation, contributions to which are deductible for federal income tax purposes under Section 170(c)(2) of the Code.

It is intended that the corporation shall have, and continue to have, the status of an organization which is exempt from federal income taxation under Sections 501(a) and 501(c)(3) of the Code. All terms and provisions of these Articles of Incorporation and the Bylaws of the Corporation, and all authority and operations of the Corporation, shall be construed, applied and carried out in accordance with such intent.

ARTICLE V
BOARD OF DIRECTORS
The Board of Directors shall have general charge of the affairs and any property and assets of the Corporation. It shall be the duty of the Directors to carry out the purposes and functions of the Corporation. The Directors shall be elected in accordance with the Bylaws of the Corporation and shall have the powers and duties set forth in these Articles of Incorporation and in the Bylaws, to the extent that such powers and duties are not inconsistent with the status of the Corporation as a nonprofit corporation, which is exempt from federal income taxation under Sections 501(a) and 501(c)(3) of the Code.

The initial Board of Directors shall be
President/ Executive Director
      Vice President / Director

Secretary

ARTICLE VI
MEMBERS

The Corporation shall have no members.

ARTICLE VII
DISSOLUTION OF CORPORATION

Upon dissolution of the Corporation, the Board of Directors shall, after paying or making provision for payment of all the liabilities of the Corporation, dispose of all of the assets of the Corporation by distributing those assets exclusively for the purposes of the Corporation in such manner, or to such organization or organizations organized and operated exclusively for public charitable uses and purposes as shall at the time qualify as exempt from taxation under Sections 501(a) and 501(c)(3) of the Code as the Board of Directors shall determine. Any such assets not so disposed of shall be disposed of by a court of competent jurisdiction for the county in which the principal office of the Corporation is then located, exclusively for such purposes or to such organization or organizations as said court shall determine, which are organized and operated exclusively for such purposes.

ARTICLE VIII
REGISTERED OFFICE AND AGENT

The initial registered agent of the Corporation shall be ABC JONES and the initial registered office shall be in DeKalb County, Georgia at 123 Lakeview GA 30316.

ARTICLE IX
LIMITATIONS ON DIRECTOR LIABILITY'
No director of the Corporation shall be liable to the Corporation for monetary damages for any action taken, or any failure to take any action, as a director, except liability (i) for any appropriation, in violation of his or her duties, of any business opportunity of the

Corporation; (ii) for acts or omissions which involve intentional misconduct or a knowing violation of the law; (iii) of the type set forth in Sections 14-3-860 through 14-3-864 of the Georgia Nonprofit Corporation Code; or (iv) for any transaction from which the director received an improper personal benefit. If the Georgia Nonprofit Corporation Code is amended after the effective date of these Articles to authorize corporate action further limiting the personal liability of directors, then the liability of a director of the Corporation shall be limited to the fullest extent permitted by the Georgia Nonprofit Corporation Code, as so amended. Any repeal or modification of the foregoing paragraph shall not adversely affect any right or protection of a director of the Corporation existing at the time of such repeal or modification.

ARTICLE X
INDEMNIFICATION; INSURANCE
(a) No director or officer of the Corporation shall be liable for any debts or obligations of the Corporation, and creditors shall look only to the assets of the Corporation for satisfaction of any debts or obligations of the Corporation.
(b) To the fullest extent permitted by applicable law, the Corporation shall indemnify any person who was or is a party or is threatened to be made a party to any threatened, pending, or completed action, suit, or proceeding, whether civil, criminal, administrative or investigative (other than (i) in connection with a proceeding by or in the right of the Corporation or (ii) in connection with any other proceeding in which the person was adjudged liable on the basis that personal benefit was improperly received by the person, whether or not involving action in the person's official capacity) by reason of the fact that he or she is or was a director, officer, employee or agent of the Corporation, or is or was serving at the request of the Corporation as a Board of Directors member, officer, employee, or agent of another corporation, partnership, joint venture, trust or other enterprise, against reasonable expenses (including attorneys' fees), judgments, fines and amounts paid in settlement actually and reasonably incurred by him or her in connection with such action, suit, or proceeding if he or she conducted himself or herself in good faith and if he or she reasonably believed (i) in the case of conduct in his or her official capacity, that

such conduct was in the best interests of the Corporation; (ii) in all other cases, that such conduct was at least not opposed to the best interests of the Corporation; and (iii) in the case of any criminal proceeding, that the individual had no reasonable cause to believe such conduct was unlawful. The termination of any action, suit, or proceeding by judgment, order, settlement, conviction, or upon a plea of nolo contendere or its equivalent, shall not, in and of itself, create a presumption that a person did not act in a manner which he or she believed in good faith to be in or not opposed to the best interests of the Corporation, and, with respect to any criminal action or proceeding, had reasonable cause to believe that his or her conduct was unlawful.

(c) To the fullest extent permitted by applicable law, the Corporation shall indemnify any person who was or is a party or is threatened to be made a party to any threatened, pending, or completed action, suit or proceeding by or in the right of the Corporation by reason of the fact he or she is or was a director, officer, employee, or agent of the Corporation, or is or was serving at the request of the Corporation as a Board of Directors member, officer, employee, or agent of another Corporation, partnership, joint venture, trust or other enterprise, against reasonable expenses only (including attorneys' fees) actually and reasonably incurred by him or her in connection with such action, suit or proceeding if it is determined that he or she conducted himself or herself in good faith and if he or she reasonably believed (i) in the case of conduct in his or her official capacity, that such conduct was in the best interests of the Corporation; (ii) in all other cases, that such conduct was at least not opposed to the best interests of the Corporation; and (iii) in the case of any criminal proceeding, that the individual had no reasonable cause to believe such conduct was unlawful. The termination of any action, suit, or proceeding by judgment, order, settlement, conviction, or upon a plea of nolo contendere or its equivalent, shall not, in and of itself, create a presumption that a person did not act in a manner which he or she believed in good faith to be in or not opposed to the best interests of the Corporation, and, with respect to any criminal action or proceeding, had reasonable cause to believe that his or her conduct was unlawful.

(d) To the extent that a person indemnified under this Article has been successful on the merits or otherwise in defense of any action, suit, or proceeding referred to in sections (b) and (c) above, or in defense of any claim, issue, or matter therein, he or she shall be indemnified against expenses (including attorneys' fees) actually and reasonably incurred by him/her in connection therewith.

(e) Any indemnification under section (b) and (c) of this Article shall be made by the Corporation only as authorized in the specific proceeding upon a determination that indemnification of the director, officer, employee, or agent is proper in the circumstances because he/she has met the applicable standard of conduct set forth in sections (b) and (c) of this Article. Such determination shall be made (i) if there are two or more disinterested directors, by the Board of Directors by a majority vote of all the disinterested directors (a majority of whom shall for such purpose constitute a quorum) or by a majority of the members of a committee of two or more disinterested directors appointed by such a vote, or (ii) if such a quorum is not obtainable, or, even if obtainable if a quorum of disinterested Board of Directors members so directs, by independent legal counsel.

(f) Expenses incurred in defending a civil or criminal action, suit, or proceeding shall, to the fullest extent permitted by law, be paid by the corporation in advance of the final disposition of such action, suit, or proceeding upon receipt of (i) a written affirmation of the director, officer, employee, or agent of his or her good faith belief that he or she has met the standard of conduct set forth herein or that the proceeding involves conduct for which liability has been eliminated and (ii) with a written undertaking by or on behalf of the director, officer, employee, or agent to repay such amount if it is ultimately determined that such person is not entitled to indemnification.

(g) The indemnification provided by this Article shall not be deemed exclusive of any other rights, in respect of the indemnification or otherwise, to which those seeking indemnification may be entitled under any Bylaw or resolution approved by the affirmative vote of the Board of Directors members taken at a meeting the notice of which specified that such Bylaw or resolution would be placed before the Board members, both as to action by a director, officer, employee, or agent in his or her official capacity and as to action in another capacity while holding such office or position, and shall continue as to a person who has ceased to be a director, officer, employee, or agent and shall inure to the benefit of the heirs, executors, and administrators of such a person. The indemnification provided by this Article shall be considered a contract right of the covered person.

(h) The Corporation and its officers shall have the power to purchase and maintain insurance on behalf of any person who is or was a director, officer, employee, or agent of the Corporation, or is or was serving at the request of the corporation as a Board member, officer, employee, or agent of another corporation, partnership, joint venture, trust or other enterprise, against any liability asserted against him or her and incurred by him or her in any such capacity, or arising out of his or her status as such, whether or not the Corporation would have the power to indemnify him or her against such liability under the provisions of this Article.

ARTICLE XI
DEFINITIONS

(a) For purposes of these Articles of Incorporation, "charitable purposes and uses" include charitable, religious, educational, literary, or scientific purposes within the meaning of Section 501(c)(3) of the Code, contributions for which are deductible under Section 170(c)(2) of the Code.

(b) All references in these Articles of Incorporation to sections of the "Internal Revenue Code" shall be considered references to the Internal Revenue Code of 1986, as from time to time amended, and to the corresponding provisions of any applicable future United States Internal Revenue Law, and to all Treasury Regulations issued under such sections and provisions.

ARTICLE XII
INCORPORATOR

The name and address of the Incorporator is Sample incorporator name, Atlanta, GA 30316
ARTICLE XIII
MAILING ADDRESS

The mailing address of the initial principal office of the corporation is

IN WITNESS WHEREOF, the undersigned has executed these Articles of Incorporation as of this _____ day of _____, 2017.

_____
ABC Jones, Incorporator

Figure 3

BYLAWS
OF
SAMPLE NONPROFIT

The name of the organization is Sample Nonprofit. The organization is organized in accordance with the Georgia Nonprofit Corporation Code, as amended. The organization has not been formed for the making of any profit, or personal financial gain. The assets and income of the organization shall not be distributable to, or benefit the trustees, directors, or officers or other individuals. The assets and income shall only be used to promote corporate purposes as described below. Nothing contained herein, however, shall be deemed to prohibit the payment of reasonable compensation to employees and independent contractors for services provided for the benefit of the organization. This organization shall not carry on any other activities not permitted to be carried on by an organization exempt from federal income tax. The organization shall not endorse, contribute to, work for, or otherwise support (or oppose) a candidate for public office. The organization is organized exclusively for purposes subsequent to section 501c3 of the Internal Revenue Code.

ARTICLE I
MEETINGS

Section 1. Annual Meeting. An annual meeting shall be held once each calendar year for electing directors and for the transaction of such other business as may properly come before the meeting. The annual meeting shall be held at the time and place designated by the Board of Directors from time to time.

Section 2. Special Meetings. Special meetings may be requested by the President or the Board of Directors.

Section 3. Notice. Written notice of all meetings, whether regular or special meetings, shall be provided under this section or as otherwise required by law. The Notice shall state the place, date, and hour of meeting, and if for a special meeting, the purpose of the meeting. Such notice shall be mailed to all directors of record at the address shown on the corporate books, at least 10 days prior to the meeting. Such notice shall be deemed effective when deposited in ordinary U.S. mail, properly addressed, with postage prepaid.

Section 4. Place of Meeting. Meetings shall be held at the organization's principal place of business unless otherwise stated in the notice. Shareholders of any class or series may participate in any meeting of shareholders by means of remote communication to the extent the Board of Directors authorizes such participation for such class or series. Participation by means of remote communication shall be subject to such guidelines and procedures as the Board of Directors adopts. Shareholders participating in a shareholders' meeting by means of remote communication shall be deemed present and may vote at such a meeting if the corporation has implemented reasonable measures: (1) to verify that each person participating remotely is a shareholder, and (2) to provide such shareholders a reasonable opportunity to participate in the meeting and to vote on matters submitted to the shareholders, including an opportunity to communicate, and to read or hear the proceedings of the meeting, substantially concurrent with such proceedings.

Section 5. Quorum. Most of the directors shall constitute a quorum at a meeting. In the absence of a quorum, a majority of the directors may adjourn the meeting to another time without further notice. If a quorum is represented at an adjourned meeting, any business may be transacted that might have been transacted at the meeting as originally scheduled. The directors present at a meeting represented by a quorum may continue to transact business until adjournment, even if the withdrawal of some directors results in representation of less than a quorum.

Section 6. Informal Action. Any action required to be taken, or which may be taken, at a meeting, may be taken without a meeting and without prior notice if a consent in writing, setting forth the action so taken, is signed by the directors with respect to the subject matter of the vote.

ARTICLE II
DIRECTORS

Section 1. Number of Directors. The organization shall be managed by a Board of Directors consisting of 3 director(s).

Section 2. Election and Term of Office. The directors shall be elected at the annual meeting. Each director shall serve a term of 1 year(s), or until a successor has been elected and qualified.

Section 3. Quorum. A majority of directors shall constitute a quorum.

Section 4. Adverse Interest. In the determination of a quorum of the directors, or in voting, the disclosed adverse interest of a director shall not disqualify the director or invalidate his or her vote.

Section 5. Regular Meeting. The Board of Directors shall meet immediately after the election for the purpose of electing its new officers, appointing new committee chairpersons and for transacting such other business as may be deemed appropriate. The Board of Directors may provide, by resolution, for additional regular meetings without notice other than the notice provided by the resolution.

Section 6. Special Meeting. Special meetings may be requested by the President, Vice-President, Secretary, or any two directors by providing five days' written notice by ordinary United States mail, effective when mailed. Minutes of the meeting shall be sent to the Board of Directors within two weeks after the meeting.

Section 7. Procedures. The vote of a majority of the directors present at a properly called meeting at which a quorum is present shall be the act of the Board of Directors, unless the vote of a greater number is required by law or by these by-laws for a particular resolution. A director of the organization who is present at a meeting of the Board of Directors at which action on any corporate matter is taken shall be presumed to have assented to the action taken unless their dissent shall be entered in the minutes of the meeting. The Board shall keep written minutes of its proceedings in its permanent records.

If authorized by the governing body, any requirement of a written ballot shall be satisfied by a ballot submitted by electronic transmission, provided that any such electronic transmission must either set forth or be submitted with information from which it can be determined that the electronic transmission was authorized by the member or proxy holder.

Section 8. Informal Action. Any action required to be taken at a meeting of directors, or any action which may be taken at a meeting of directors or of a committee of directors, may be taken without a meeting if a consent in writing setting forth the action so taken, is signed by all of the directors or all of the members of the committee of directors, as the case may be.

Section 9. Removal / Vacancies. A director shall be subject to removal, with or without cause, at a meeting called for that purpose. Any vacancy that occurs on the Board of Directors, whether by death, resignation, removal or any other cause, may be filled by the remaining directors. A director elected to fill a vacancy shall serve the remaining term of his or her predecessor, or until a successor has been elected and qualified.

Section 10. Resignation. Any director may resign effective upon giving written notice to the chairperson of the board, the president, the secretary or the Board of Directors of the corporation, unless the notice specifies a later time for the effectiveness of such resignation. If the resignation is effective at a future time, a successor may be elected to take office when the resignation becomes effective.

Section 11. Committees. To the extent permitted by law, the Board of Directors may appoint from its members a committee or committees, temporary or permanent, and designate the duties, powers and authorities of such committees.

ARTICLE III
OFFICERS

Section 1. Number of Officers. The officers of the organization shall be a President, one or more Vice-Presidents (as determined by the Board of Directors), and a Secretary. Two or more offices may be held by one person

President/Chairman. The President shall be the chief executive officer and shall preside at all meetings of the Board of Directors and its Executive Committee, if such a committee is created by the Board.

Vice President. The Vice President shall perform the duties of the President in the absence of the President and shall assist that office in the discharge of its leadership duties.

Secretary. The Secretary shall give notice of all meetings of the Board of Directors and Executive Committee, if any, shall keep an accurate list of the directors, and shall have the authority to certify any records, or copies of records, as the official records of the organization. The Secretary shall maintain the minutes of the Board of Directors' meetings and all committee meetings.

Section 2. Election and Term of Office. The officers shall be elected annually by the Board of Directors at the first meeting of the Board of Directors, immediately following the annual meeting. Each officer shall serve a one year term or until a successor has been elected and qualified.

Section 3. Removal or Vacancy. The Board of Directors shall have the power to remove an officer or agent of the organization. Any vacancy that occurs for any reason may be filled by the Board of Directors.

ARTICLE IV
CORPORATE SEAL, EXECUTION OF INSTRUMENTS

The organization shall not have a corporate seal. All instruments that are executed on behalf of the organization which are acknowledged and which affect an interest in real estate shall be executed by the President or any Vice-President and the Secretary or Treasurer. All other instruments executed by the organization, including a release of mortgage or lien, may be executed by the President or any Vice-President. Notwithstanding the preceding provisions of this section, any written instrument may be executed by any officer(s) or agent(s) that are specifically designated by resolution of the Board of Directors.

ARTICLE V
AMENDMENT TO BYLAWS

The bylaws may be amended, altered, or repealed by the Board of Directors by a two-thirds majority of a quorum vote at any regular or special meeting.

ARTICLE VI
DISSOLUTION

The organization may be dissolved only with authorization of its Board of Directors given at a special meeting called for that purpose, and with the subsequent approval by no less than two-thirds (2/3) vote of the members. In the event of the dissolution of the organization, the assets shall be applied and distributed as follows:

All liabilities and obligations shall be paid, satisfied and discharged, or adequate provision shall be made therefore. Assets not held upon a condition requiring return, transfer, or conveyance to any other organization or individual shall be distributed, transferred, or conveyed, in trust or otherwise, to charitable and educational organization, organized under Section 501(c)(3) of the Internal Revenue Code of 1986, as amended, of a similar or like nature to this organization, as determined by the Board of Directors.

Certification

Sample Secretary Name, Secretary of Sample Nonprofit hereby certifies that the foregoing is a true and correct copy of the bylaws of the above-named organization, duly adopted by the initial Board of Directors on _____.

_____

Sample Secretary Signature
Figure 4

CHAPTER 3 LET'S GET FEDERAL

Now that you have completed all of your necessary paperwork at the state level, it is time to move onto the Federal level. This is where you begin to implement governmental benefits that will allow you to position yourself as a player in the game. Corporations want to make sure they are in business with companies that have taken the time to legitimize themselves. This shows you are serious and professional about your business. This also, minimizes the chance there could be ramifications from dealing with a company that hasn't taken the time to ensure they are operating within the parameters of the law. Your reputation is everything as a small nonprofit business. You must work harder and longer than more established businesses because you are the new kid on the block.

You are now upon a pivotal moment in this process; continue to give yourself and God an #unconditionalYES. What that means is no matter what it looks like., no matter how tough it gets you will not give excuses as to why you are not walking it out. There will be times that seem like it is impossible. However, those are the times your faith has to level up to the size of your dreams. You can't expect to achieve million dollar donors and sponsors on faith for payment of your car note. Greater the destiny, greater the faith regard to accomplish it. It never seems like the right time when you are pushing toward your destiny. There will always be something unexpected that comes up, it comes just to remove your focus from the task at hand. I am not telling you this is going to be easy. Success is never easy, ask anyone that has ever done anything in excellence. Read any great man or woman's biography, it is filled with stories of adversity, faith, strength and tenacity. These are characterizations of all average people accomplishing extraordinary task. There is greatness in you just keep pushing. Think about getting you an accountability partner. That is someone who will continue to hold you accountable for completing your task and motivating you when you seem like you have been caught in the middle of the water, you can't see land and you can't turn back. AP partners work! I have several AP partners. Also, pray daily it helps clear your mind on days it seems cloudy, overwhelmed and unsure.

You should be excited at this point! It is important to take a moment to acknowledge your accomplishments. Often, we work so hard toward our goals and never stop to appreciate how far we have come. You have walked out your **#unconditionalYES™** up to this point, and it has yielded results.

Ok, here we are at the Federal Level, we are approaching the last leg of legitimizing your nonprofit on a whole other level. You will be filing online. It is quicker and guided, which equates to a simpler process all around for you. Go to www.irs.gov you will be filing for your EIN (finally, something that doesn't cost money). The purpose of an **E**mployer **I**dentification **N**umber is for tax administration. Search for IRS Form SS-4 **online filing,** do not print and mail**.** This should take less than 15 minutes and it is absolutely free. You will need a copy of your paperwork from your state filing to assist with the internet EIN. This is a guided online questionnaire you will only need to fill in the blanks with the assistance of your state paperwork. Your EIN can be utilized immediately. The EIN is necessary to open your corporate bank account. Please note it will take up to two weeks before your EIN can pass an IRS taxpayer number matching program. (This is relevant if you are setting up an aspect of your business and the verification process is automated for determining your EIN is legally registered). The EIN will not delay the filing of your 1023EZ.

Make a reminder to self: Nearly all organizations exempt under IRC 501(a) are subject to automatic revocation of their tax-exempt status if they fail to file a required annual information return or notice for three consecutive years. When you apply for an EIN, it is presumed you're legally formed and the clock starts running on this three-year period.

Congratulations! Another step completed. I pray you are feeling pretty good about what you have accomplished. Keeping giving your

#unconditionalYES™. Things are already changing. There should be an increased level of excitement. You are bringing to life your purpose. You have now moved from dreamer to doer. Every step places you closer to fulfilling your goals.

You should be simultaneously working on your business plan and mission statement. The SBA has a wonderful template that will store your business plan, provide easy prompting questions and it will save it as you develop your plan. Take care to develop a well thought out mission statement. It is important to have a mission statement that speaks to what your organization represents in less than fifteen words. The top fifty mission statements from the top nonprofits are all under twenty-nine words with the top eighteen being ten words and under. I hope you get the idea. Your mission statement should not turn into your company vision statement. They are two distinct items. You want your mission statement to be easily memorable, it should inform, provide your company focuses as well as peaks the interest in your organization. As a nonprofit you will continuously be asked about your company mission. You will need that famous two-minute elevator pitch as you will frequently be asked the question, what is your nonprofit? Make sure you memorize it. It may make the difference between getting the sponsorships or not. Often when you are networking people no longer have a long attention span due to our love of the microwave world of social media, you must be concise, short and memorable simultaneously.

CHAPTER 4 THE 501©3

It seems like everything you're doing takes money. Well get comfortable with that. You are in the charitable business you will constantly find well-meaning reasons to expend money and solicit from donors for you to expend more money. Seek wisdom and become prudent with your funds now. If you are not one that likes to create budgets take a class, view a YouTube or employ someone to help you establish budgetary parameters for your organization. It takes a great deal of finances to operate a non-profit organization. In order to have a lasting business you must seek great counsel and budget at an even greater level. Once a 501©3 has been granted it is important to establish excellent record keeping routines. This will assist in establishing accurate records to provide once you began to seek out larger grants. Start your business out on the right foot and you won't find yourself trying to double back to correct things when the perfect opportunity comes along.

Time to complete the paperwork for the 501(c)(3).

This is an investment (remember you have given God and yourself an **#unconditionalYES**™), *plus you have made provisions to start your business. If money is an issue—get creative. Have a yard sale, ask your family and friends to donate items you can sell. Give up your favorite coffee or smoothie and make it at home. Take on extra hours at work or get a part time job. You must be willing to make the sacrifices now to achieve the desired result.*

What is a 501©3?

Being a registered **501(c)(3)** means that the Internal Revenue Service (IRS) has designated you as an approved nonprofit tax-exempt charitable organization. "Charitable" is broadly-defined as being established for purposes that are religious, educational, charitable, scientific, social literary, testing for public safety, fostering of national or international amateur sports, or prevention of cruelty to animals and children.

Why become 501©3?

One of the primary benefits of being tax-exempt under IRC Section 501(c)(3) is the ability to accept contributions and donations that are tax-deductible to the donor. Additional benefits include, but are not limited to the following:

- Exemption from federal and/or state corporate income taxes.

- Possible exemption from state sales and property taxes (*varies by state). Once property is purchased by a nonprofit organization, it must reside permanently with a nonprofit.

- Ability to apply for grants and other public or private allocations available only to IRS-recognized, 501(c)(3) organizations.

- Potentially higher thresholds before incurring federal and/or state unemployment tax liabilities.

- The public legitimacy of IRS recognition.

- Discounts on US Postal bulk-mail rates and other services.

Does nonprofit, 501(c)(3) and tax-exempt all mean the same thing?

Actually, no! These terms are often used interchangeably, but they all mean different things. Nonprofit means the entity, usually a corporation, is organized for a nonprofit purpose. 501(c)(3) means a nonprofit organization that has been recognized by the IRS as being tax-exempt by virtue of its charitable programs. Tax-exemption is the result of a nonprofit organization being recognized by the IRS as being organized for any purpose allowable under 501(c)(3) - 501(c)(27). For our purpose of a nonprofit business, we utilize 501(c)(3).

What form is required to get 501(c)(3) status?

To obtain designation as a 501(c)(3), tax-exempt entity, **Form 1023** must be filed with the Internal Revenue Service. Form 1023 is a 29-page, comprehensive look at an organization's structure and programs. Given the number of additional schedules, attachments and exhibits that may be required in addition to the application itself, most Form 1023 filings range between 50-100 pages of information.

Form 1023-EZ is a much more generalized document that does not require written budgets or narratives. Form 1023-EZ is specifically designed for certain, low-budget organizations. This is my recommendation for beginning organizations with smaller budgets.
The new Form 1023-EZ, available today on IRS.gov, is three pages long, compared with the standard 26-page Form 1023. Most small organizations, including as many as 70 percent of all applicants, qualify to use the new streamlined form. Most organizations with gross receipts of $50,000 or less and assets of $250,000 or less are eligible. After approval, you will receive your determination letter, which consist of your tax-exempt number and your EIN. You can find this online form at ww.pay.gov

How much is the user fee for an exemption application?
The user fee for an organization filing Form 1023 is $600.

This is the avenue most small nonprofits will take
*If the organization is eligible to submit Form 1023-EZ, the user fee is $275.

The fee must be paid through www.pay.gov when the application is filed. These amounts are subject to change; the IRS publishes the latest user fee information at www.IRS.gov, keyword "user fee";

Drum Roll Please! Approval time is only 2-4 weeks with 1023EZ

CHAPTER 5 MONEY, MONEY, MONEY

I am sure this section is what you have been waiting for or maybe even thumbed through to read first. We all want to know how do I get the money? Where are all those grants I hear spoken about all the time? Lead me to all that wonderful free money I hear people talking about. You have probable already started looking for a grant writer or looked at a few classes on learning how to become a grant writer. We all have fantasized and dreamed of starting a nonprofit and getting **"The Grant**", that government money that will fund your dream. You know the "one" grant you believe will take care of all our expenses. Well I am not sure how to break the news. Let me just rip the band aid off now! WAKE UP!!!, that is just a dream, a rumor, fake news whatever phrase you want to plug in. Yes, there are funds but let's go over the very basic requirements you will need as a **small business nonprofit** to begin to get those multimillion dollar grants the government brags so much about.

Don't get scammed out of your hard-earned money by paying for a grant writer and you haven't even taken in your first client, or serviced the community in any way.

Here are your basic requirements for a grant, specifically from any government entity.

- **3 years of documented financial records.**

They want to see how you have handled your funds prior to the grant. No one is going to give you a substantial amount of money without some type of financial accountability. This is their investment into you and what you are doing.

That's like going to buy a house and they don't see if you are credit worthy and

43

can afford the house. Make sure you document well and always operate with a high level of integrity and excellence not matter how small you are. Remember you are a giant they just don't know it yet!

- **A business plan**

It takes time to build a solid business plan. Take your time you have a little bit of time before you qualify for any major grants. Take a few classes on writing a well put together business plan. The SBA is a fantastic resource for gaining a wealth of information regarding small business knowledge. Remember, you are in this for long term success.

- **A proven model**

A proven model means they want to certain that you are not going to fly from the seat of your pants and waste their money. They are making an investment in you. Take the time to work out any flaws in your initial program. Once you begin implementing these programs you will see that it will become necessary to adjust. This becomes your working model. The longer you do this the more data you will be able to provide to support your readiness to expand your capacity in preparation for your next level with grants. Whatever area you have decided to focus on in the nonprofit sector be prepared to become creative in how you raise money initially to implement your programs.

These are just the most basic reasons to not run out and listen to the first person asking for a ton of money to write a grant to realize you don't qualify, yet.

Don't get disappointed. Realize there is a lot of money out there. You will have to work hard and continue to give your **#unconditionalYES™**. Remember you are doing this because this is part of your destiny and purpose. This isn't a hobby. You are changing lives and following the command of God on your life. Success is never easy, but it is worth it to change and enhance your legacy, to bring change to the world. This is your opportunity to become a history maker. Everyday ordinary people do extraordinary things. I am here to tell you I believe you can achieve the extraordinary things in life by persevering, don't let no become a deterrent. Never see a plan that doesn't work out as a failure see it has an option that has been ruled out and the opportunity to gain wisdom in your field. This part of the job takes determination and the ability to deal with a ton of no's just to get the one yes.

Let's go get us some money…

The easiest grants to qualify for are **community grants**. Look around and you can find those everywhere. Most often, they are small scale grants ranging from $500 to $5,000, which does not require the promise your first-born child. To locate these, you need only look around your own neighborhood. Any business is a potential donor. Seek out businesses that align with your vision and mission statement. These organizations have a higher probability of saying yes. For example, you do not want to request funding from a pet store to help cloth and feed homeless people. If you have an animal rescue you have a better chance for approval. You must be prepared with your plan of action for the funds, a copy of your 501©3 determination letter and at least four to six weeks before you require the funds.

Register with TechSoup at www.techsoup.org, a nonprofit organization that serves as the gatekeeper for many large companies that do want to help others, but do not want the administrative headache of verifying your **501(c)(3)** status.

Sign up with Good360, https://good360.org/ and add the alerts. They often provide donated goods for free. Ex. Party City donated thousands of items through Good360.

Job Matching is another great source of donor revenue. Many companies will match their employees' contribution to your organization. The next time someone donates ask them if their job matches contributions. It's an easy way to double your donation.

There are many creative ways to support your organization. Fundraising, Corporate Giving, Yard Sales, Friends and Family, Social Media, Crowd Funding, i.e. Gofund Me.

Here are a few Do's and Don'ts

- **Don't** get caught in the grant websites that offer grants
- **Do** file for your Duns and Bradstreet number it is mandatory if you plan on securing any funding from the government www.dnb.com.
- **Don't** be tempted to purchase any additional service yet from Dun and Bradstreet. Maybe when you have a budget that will allow the additional expense. It is an unnecessary expense in the infantile state of your organization.
- **Do** Register your organization with grants.gov and SAMS
- **Do** keep your business safe on the internet, don't fall prey to grant scams promising things for money.
- **Don't** rely solely on grants and donations to fund your organization!

Reflection

Take a moment to review what you've learned and
to write down your thoughts and ideas.

_____

_____

_____

_____

_____

_____

_____

_____

_____

What ideas have you come up with to creatively fund your
organization initially?

_____

_____

_____

_____

_____

_____

_____

_____

Have you decided to give your life's purpose and journey and **#unconditionalYES™?** What does that look like and what steps are you planning to take to implement a lifestyle that reflects a no excuse, #unconditionalYES mentality?

_____

_____

_____

_____

_____

_____

_____

_____

_____

I believe you have just stepped into another aspect of your destiny and purpose. Nothing will stop you from achieving your dream. Life will bring you unexpected events but don't let life's delays be your excuse to not continually run toward your destiny. It doesn't matter the pace. What matters is you still forge ahead. One day you will look behind you and see just how far you've come. NEVER GIVE UP! This life is yours for the taking. You were born to make a difference in this world. May God Bless you and keep you! Always remember to give your life an

#unconditionalYES™.

Work Hard!

Give an #UnconditionalYES!

Never Give Up!

You Were Made for This!

My webinar is available quarterly and goes into extensive detail regarding who is giving out those great community grants and how to secure a six-figure lucrative marketing grant with a billion-dollar company. Who doesn't need free marketing? You see all those sponsor ads in Facebook, Instagram, Google and YouTube. Don't think marketing isn't a key component in your business. I also (in real time) visit the websites on the state and federal level along with going directly to community grant sites to show you how to apply. Also, you will have an opportunity to submit your questions to a panel of experts.

You can register for the class at www.risenlightened.org

My nonprofit organization Running In Stilettoes Enlightened, focuses on domestic violence and sexual abuse. I provide classes and resources to assist survivors with regaining their voice, overcoming trauma and seeking out their purpose to pursue with passion. Take a moment to look at my site, make a donation or refer a friend. Great businesses are made through great partnerships and connections. Let's be great together!

I frequently speak on topics such as

- Living an #unconditionalYES Life
- Regaining Your Voice – Healing from the Abuse
- Help! I Wanna Start a Nonprofit

For booking info. email rcmarshall@risenlightened.org

Find me on social media

RC Marshall

R.C. Marshall

Works Citations

(irs.gov/charities-non-profits, 2018)
(SBA, 2018)
(Rocket Lawyer, 2018)

ABOUT THE AUTHOR

R.C. Marshall is the Founder of Running in Stilettoes Enlightened a women's nonprofit organization. Running in Stilettoes Enlightened assist women with overcoming the adversities associated with domestic and sexual abuse. The mission of Running in Stilettoes Enlightened is to Propel abused women to R.I.S.E. above Spiritual, Emotional and Physical Wounds to Restore Wholeness and Joy. R.C. is also a Prophetic Intercessor. She has traveled internationally to speak to women and spread the good news of Jesus Christ. She has held various leadership positions within the local church, currently she is a member of Kingdom Builders Church in Conyers, GA. She studied at Liberty University majoring in psychology. R.C.'s passions are prayer, intercession, and educating, coupled with encouraging women through the lens of the scripture to help women discover who they are in Christ. Her family has been in the nonprofit sector for over fifteen years. Giving of her time and talent so people would find their way to God is why she was born.

www.ingramcontent.com/pod-product-compliance
Lightning Source LLC
Chambersburg PA
CBHW071239220526
45468CB00002B/925